"Better Day Books," the floral book logo, and "It's a Good Day to Have a Better Day" are trademarks of Better Day Books, Inc.

"Schiffer," "Schiffer Publishing, Ltd.," and the pen and inkwell logo are registered trademarks of Schiffer Publishing, Ltd.

Illustration by Jessie Arnold
Book design by Michael Douglas

ISBN: 978-0-7643-6298-9
Printed in India
5 4 3 2
Copublished by Better Day Books and Schiffer Publishing, Ltd.

BETTER DAY BOOKS™

SCHIFFER
PUBLISHING

Schiffer Publishing, Ltd.
4880 Lower Valley Road
Atglen, PA 19310
Phone: 610-593-1777
Fax: 610-593-2002
E-mail: Info@schifferbooks.com
Web: www.schifferbooks.com

This title is available for promotional or commercial use, including special editions. Contact info@schifferbooks.com for more information.

# TRUST me YOU CAN DRAW

Mrs. Arnold

JESSIE ARNOLD

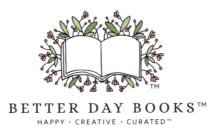

BETTER DAY BOOKS™

HAPPY · CREATIVE · CURATED™

# CONTENTS

## Welcome!

## Getting Started

## CHAPTER 1: COLOR

Page 22

TRUST ME, YOU CAN DRAW

# CHAPTER 2: DRAW—Cute Animals

# CHAPTER 2: DRAW–Nature

**Acorn & Pine Cone · Page 55**

**Bee & Hive · Page 56**

**Bird · Page 57**

**Birdhouse · Page 58**

**Butterflies · Page 59**

**Cactus · Page 60**

**Dragonfly & Ladybug · Page 61**

**Flowers · Page 62**

**Gnome · Page 63**

**Leaf · Page 64**

**Mushroom · Page 65**

**Pumpkin · Page 66**

**Seedlings · Page 67**

**Seed Packet · Page 68**

**Snowflakes · Page 69**

**Snowman · Page 70**

**Stems · Page 71**

**Succulents · Pages 72–73**

**Sunshine · Page 74**

**Trees · Page 75**

**Watering Can · Page 76**

# CHAPTER 2: DRAW—Food

# CHAPTER 2: DRAW—Super Fun PAGES 102–125

Banners · Page 103

Baseball Glove · Page 104

Boom Box · Page 105

Camper · Page 106

Clouds · Page 107

Crayon · Page 108

Envelope & Letter · Page 109

Feather · Page 110

Frames · Page 111

Gemstone · Page 112

House · Page 113

Lightbulb · Page 114

Moon & Star · Page 115

Paintbrushes · Page 116

Paisley · Page 117

Pencil & Sharpener · Page 118

Robot · Page 119

Rocket · Page 120

Sugar Skull · Page 121

Unicorn · Page 122

TRUST ME, YOU CAN DRAW

8

# CHAPTER 3: **LETTER**

# CHAPTER 4: **Putting It All Together**

# WELCOME TO MY ART ROOM!

I'm so glad you are here! I have been teaching art for more than twenty years. Whenever I tell someone that I am an art teacher, they always respond the same way, "I can't draw." I'm here to tell you that you can. You might need some guidance and, more importantly, practice. This book will give you step-by-step directions for drawing, lettering, and putting it all together. You'll also get some fun coloring sheets! Once you get the hang of it, you can start to develop your own style. Have fun and be creative!

*Mrs. Arnold*

# Getting STARTED

Getting started is easy! All you need
are some basic supplies, a few tips and
tricks, a little determination, and a lot
of PRACTICE! Like anything, the more
you practice, the better you will get.
Remember, your drawing style might
be different than mine, and that's okay!
Think of these instructions as building
blocks in your creative journey.
Now let's get started!

# DRAWING BASICS

All drawings and letters break down into simple lines and shapes.
Here are the ones I use most often.

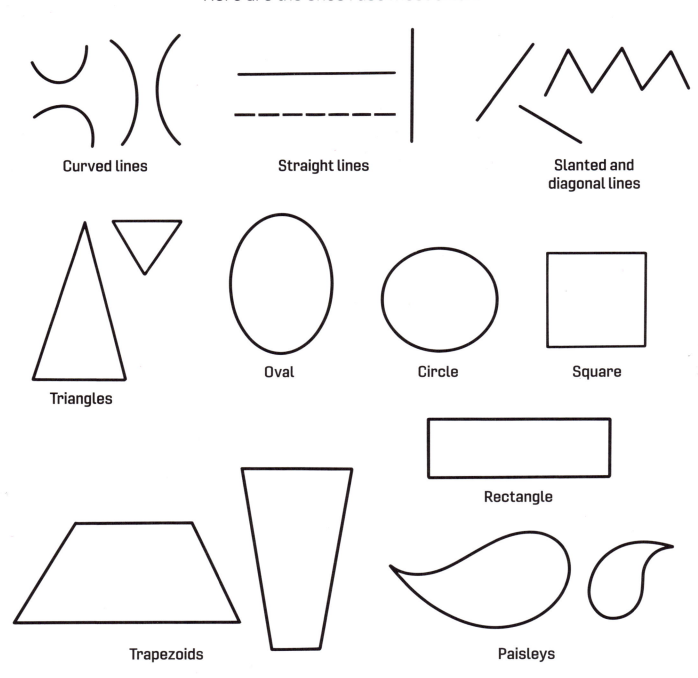

**Curved lines**

**Straight lines**

**Slanted and diagonal lines**

**Triangles**

**Oval**

**Circle**

**Square**

**Rectangle**

**Trapezoids**

**Paisleys**

14

# SUPPLIES

You don't need fancy or expensive supplies! You can purchase these supplies at most craft stores, or you might even have them already. There is plenty of room to practice in this book, but an extra sketchbook is also good to have on hand.

Pencil with eraser

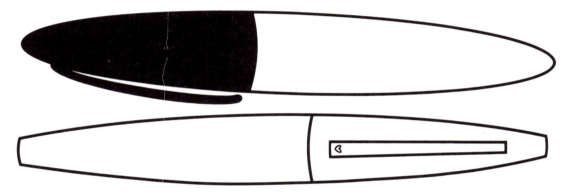

Black markers with a variety of tip sizes

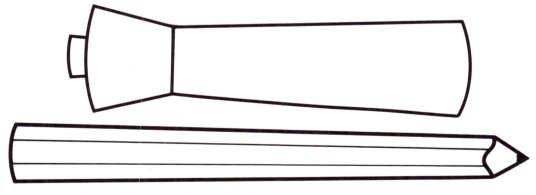

Something to color with like markers or colored pencils

# DOODLE FILLERS

I use "doodle fillers" in all of my work. These small patterns or drawings can fill empty spaces and balance drawings and letters.

**Here are my favorites:**

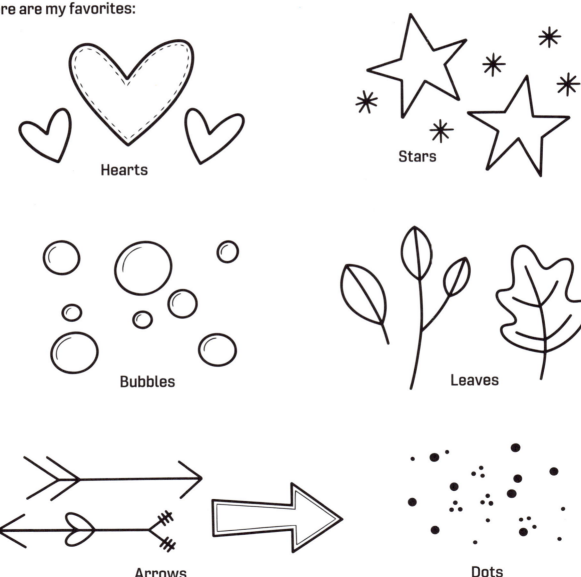

Hearts

Stars

Bubbles

Leaves

Arrows

Dots

# SHADOWS & HIGHLIGHTS

Shadows and highlights help define your work and give it a three-dimensional look. I usually add shadows and highlights to my letters. If you want to add these, you will need two additional supplies—a gray marker and a white gel pen.

When light hits an object, shadows and highlights appear. To keep it simple, imagine that the light source is coming from the top left. When that happens, the shadow falls along the bottom and right, and the highlight appears on the top left. Both the shadow and the highlight follow the shape of the object. Here is how different letter As look with shadows and highlights.

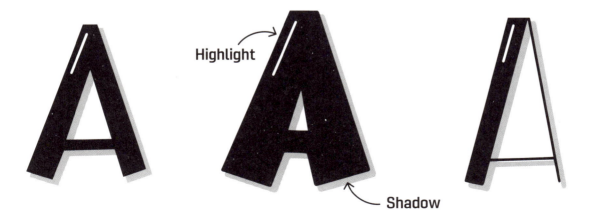

Highlight

Shadow

Coloring is a fun and relaxing activity. People of all ages enjoy this hobby! But did you know that coloring can also help increase focus, develop fine motor skills, and improve coordination? Most importantly, coloring can help encourage creativity! Don't worry about staying in the lines. Make these coloring pages unique so they reflect your personality!

DON'T KALE MY VIBE

# LET'S HANG!

LET'S ROLL!

CRAYON

MAKER'S GONNA MAKE

SCHOOL GLUE

TAKE A HIKE

CAMP

TRAIL

The easiest way to learn to draw is to break the subject down into simple lines and shapes. You will see that I use the same lines and shapes over and over. I recommend that you start drawing by sketching lightly with a pencil. When you are happy with your sketch, go over it with a marker. Use a medium tip for outlining and a fine tip for filling in small details. When you are finished, go back and erase any pencil lines that are showing.

**Happy Drawing!**

# CUTE ANIMALS

 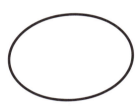

# BUNNY

**STEP 1**
Start with an oval for the head.

**STEP 2**
Draw two curved lines for the ears.
Then draw a smaller curved line inside
each one for the inner part of the ears.

**STEP 3**
Use curved lines for
the body and back leg.

**STEP 4**
Add a curved line
to finish the leg.

**STEP 5**
Draw two curved lines for
the front legs and connected
curved lines for the tail.

**STEP 6**
Add any extra
details and color.

# cAT

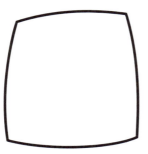

**STEP 1**
Start with a rounded square.

**STEP 2**
Add two triangles on top for the ears.

**STEP 3**
Erase any extra pencil lines.

**STEP 4**
Draw two curved lines for the face patches.

**STEP 5**
Make an oval for the nose and a curved line for the tail

**STEP 6**
Add details and color.

# CHAMELEON

**STEP 1**
Start by making a curved triangle. Leave an opening on the side.

**STEP 2**
From the side with the opening, draw a long curved line for the top of the body and the tail.

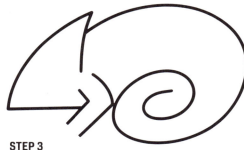

**STEP 3**
At the bottom of the triangle, add double angled lines for the leg.

**STEP 4**
Along the top curve, draw angled spikes. Draw connected triangles at the bottom of the leg for toes.

**STEP 5**
Erase any extra pencil lines and make a spotted pattern on the back.

**STEP 6**
Make a face. Add details and color.

# CHICKEN

**STEP 1**
Start with a curved trapezoid for the body.

**STEP 2**
Draw a curved line for the head.

**STEP 3**
Draw connected curved lines for the top feathers and tail.

**STEP 4**
Make a triangle for the beak and a sideways heart for the wing.

**STEP 5**
Add a small upside-down heart under the beak. Use straight lines for the legs.

**STEP 6**
Add any extra details and color.

# CRAB

### STEP 1
Start with an oval for the body.

### STEP 2

Add two small ovals for eyes and attach them to the body with straight lines.

### STEP 3
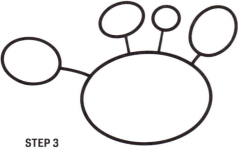
Make two more ovals for the claws and attach them to the body with straight lines.

### STEP 4
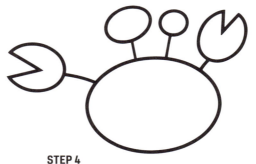
In each claw, draw a small triangle.

### STEP 5

Erase any extra pencil lines and make three long, skinny curved lines on each side for the legs.

### STEP 6

Add a face, any extra details, and color.

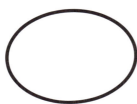

  # DOg

**STEP 1**
Start with half an oval for the head. Curve the top line.

**STEP 2**
Draw a trapezoid underneath the head for the body.

**STEP 3**
Make two ovals for ears and two curved lines for the back legs.

**STEP 4**
Draw two curved lines for the front legs.

**STEP 5**
Draw a face and make a tail with two curved lines.

**STEP 6**
Add any extra details and color.

# eLePHaNT

**STEP 1**
Start with an oval for the ear.

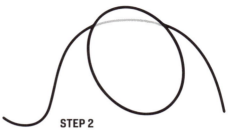

**STEP 2**
Draw a curved line behind the ear for the body. Flip the curved line up where the trunk will be.

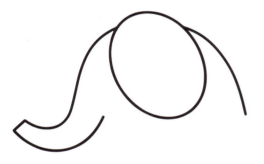

**STEP 3**
Erase any extra pencil lines. Finish the trunk with another curved line and a straight line.

**STEP 4**
Draw two rectangular shapes for the legs.

**STEP 5**
Connect the legs with a curved line for the stomach. Add two smaller rectangular shapes for the legs and a small upside-down heart for the tail.

**STEP 6**
Add any extra details and color.

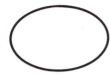 # FLAMINGO

**STEP 1**
Start with an oval for the body.

**STEP 2**
Draw three connected curved lines for the wing and tail.

**STEP 3**
Erase any extra pencil lines and make a small oval above the body for the head.

**STEP 4**
Connect the head to the body with double curved lines.

**STEP 5**
Erase any extra pencil lines.
Use curved lines for the beak and straight lines for the legs. Add a small triangle at the bottom of each leg for feet.

**STEP 6**
Add any extra details and color.

# FOX

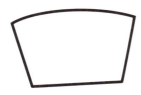

**STEP 1**
Start with a trapezoid shape for the head. Curve the top line.

**STEP 2**
Add two triangles for ears and a triangle at the bottom of the head.

**STEP 3**
Draw a paisley shape under the head for the tail.

**STEP 4**
Connect the head to the tail with diagonal lines to make the body.

**STEP 5**
Make a small oval for the nose and two curved lines for the snout. Add a zigzag line on the chest and tail.

**STEP 6**
Erase any extra pencil lines. Add details and color.

# gOLDFiSH

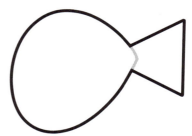

**STEP 1**
Start with a rounded teardrop shape for the body.

**STEP 2**
Draw a triangle for the tail.

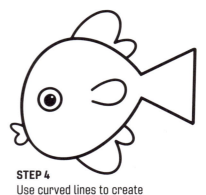

**STEP 3**
Erase any extra pencil lines and use circles to make the eye.

**STEP 4**
Use curved lines to create the fins and mouth.

**STEP 5**
Add details and color.

# ✿ HEDGEHOG ✿

**STEP 1**
Start with an oval
for the body.

**STEP 2**
Make a curved line for the head.

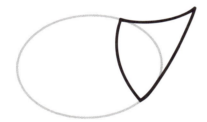

**STEP 3**
Draw two curved lines from
the oval to make the snout.

**STEP 4**
Use curved lines to create
the feet and ear.

**STEP 5**
Draw spiked lines around the
oval to complete the body.

**STEP 6**
Add details and color.

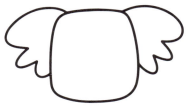

# KOALA

44

**STEP 1**
Start with a curved rectangular shape for the head.

**STEP 2**
Draw connected curved lines for the ears.

**STEP 3**
Make a curved line for the chest and a curved line for the paw.

**STEP 4**
Use a curved line for the body and bottom leg.

**STEP 5**
Draw double curved lines for the branch and two curved lines for the tail.

**STEP 6**
Add any extra details and color.

# LLAMA

**STEP 1**
Start with two ovals for
the head and body.

**STEP 2**
Make another oval for the face and
two curved lines for the horns.

**STEP 3**
Draw four skinny rectangles
for the legs.

**STEP 4**
Go over the body with curved lines
for the fur.

**STEP 5**
Erase any extra pencil lines.
Add a face, a tail, hooves, and
a curved line for the blanket.

**STEP 6**
Add details and color.

# NARWHAL

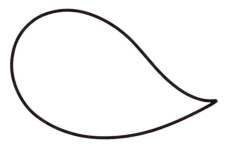

**STEP 1**
Start with a paisley shape.

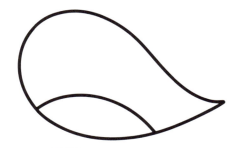

**STEP 2**
Draw a curved line for the stomach.

**STEP 3**
Make curved lines for the flippers and tail.

**STEP 4**
Draw a long, skinny triangle for the horn.

**STEP 5**
Make a spotted pattern on the body and curved lines on the horn.

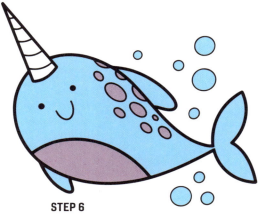

**STEP 6**
Add any extra details and color.

# OWL

**STEP 1**
Start with two touching circles.

**STEP 2**
Draw additional circles inside to make eyes.

**STEP 3**
Make an oval behind the eyes for the body.

**STEP 4**
Add curved lines to make the wings and stomach.

**STEP 5**
Draw triangles for the ears and beak and lines for the feet.

**STEP 6**
Add details and color.

# PANDA

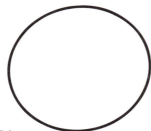

**STEP 1**
Start with a circle for the head.

**STEP 2**
Draw two ovals for the eyes and two curved lines for the ears.

**STEP 3**
Make two curved lines for the front legs.

**STEP 4**
Draw a curved line behind the front legs for the body.

**STEP 5**
Erase any extra pencil lines. Make a curved line for the back leg and a curved line for the tail.

**STEP 6**
Add any extra details and color.

# RACCOON

**STEP 1**
Start by drawing a small oval with a curved line behind it.

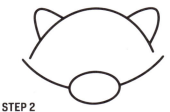

**STEP 2**
Make a slightly smaller curved line above the first and add two rounded triangles for the ears.

**STEP 3**
Draw a small oval for the nose, a rectangular base for the body, and curved lines for the back legs and stomach.

**STEP 4**
Add curved lines for the paws and tail. Make curved lines for the snout and face stripes.

**STEP 5**
Connect the top and bottom curved lines of the head with a line. Draw two ovals for the front paws.

**STEP 6**
Add any extra details and color.

# SLOTH

**STEP 1**
Start with an oval for the head.

**STEP 2**
Draw a curved line underneath for the body.

**STEP 3**
Make two ovals for the legs.

**STEP 4**
Connect the legs with a curved line.

**STEP 5**
Erase any extra pencil lines and draw a circle for the face.

**STEP 6**
Add curved lines for the face patches and draw in a face.

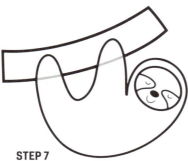

**STEP 7**
Use a curved rectangle to make a branch behind the legs.

**STEP 8**
Add details and color.

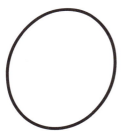 # sNAiL

**STEP 1**
Start with an oval for the shell.

**STEP 2**
Draw a curved line connected to the shell for the body.

**STEP 3**
Make two small ovals connected to the body with straight lines for the eyes.

**STEP 4**
Draw a spiral inside the shell.

**STEP 5**
Draw a face.

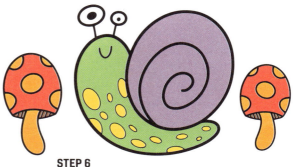

**STEP 6**
Add any extra details and color.

 # WALRUS

**STEP 1**
Start with an oval.

**STEP 2**
Make two curved lines at the bottom of the oval for the front flippers.

**STEP 3**
Use two curved lines to extend the side of the oval for the body.

**STEP 4**
Draw two curved triangles for the tail.

**STEP 5**
Make an upside-down heart for the face and two curved triangles for the tusks. Use circles for the eyes and nose.

**STEP 6**
Add details and color.

# PRACTICE

# NATURE DRAWINGS

# ACORn & Pine Cone

**Acorn**

**STEP 1**
Start with an oval for the cap.

**STEP 2**
Draw two curved lines underneath, connecting them so they come to a point at the bottom.

**STEP 3**
Add details and color.

**Pine Cone**

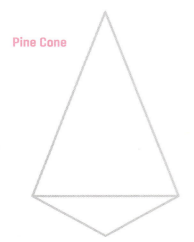

**STEP 1**
Draw an upside-down kite shape for the base.

**STEP 2**
Add overlapping curved triangles and rectangles for the scales.

**STEP 3**
Erase any extra pencil lines and color.

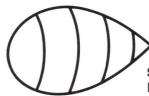 # Bee & Hive

**Bee**

### STEP 1
Start with a sideways teardrop shape.

### STEP 2
Draw curved lines for the stripes.

### STEP 3
Make a circle with a smaller circle inside for the eye.

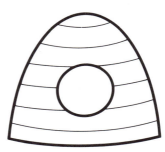

### STEP 4
Draw two curved lines for the wings and two lines for the antennae and color.

**Hive**

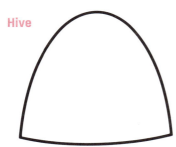

### STEP 1
Start with a curved line. Connect the bottom with another curved line.

### STEP 2
Draw a circle in the center and curved lines for the details. Color.

# BiRD

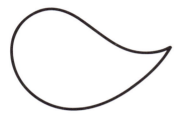

**STEP 1**
Start with a paisley shape for the body.

**STEP 2**
Draw teardrop shapes for the wing and tail.

**STEP 3**
Make a triangle for the beak and a curved line for the stomach.

**STEP 4**
Draw two straight lines for legs, a rectangle with curved ends for the branch, and an eye.

**STEP 5**
Add details and color.

  # BiRDHouse

**STEP 1**
Start with an open triangle.

**STEP 2**
Double the triangle line
for the roof.

**STEP 3**
Draw a rectangle connected to
the roof for the bottom of the
house and a circle for the opening.

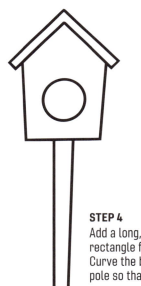

**STEP 4**
Add a long, skinny
rectangle for the pole.
Curve the bottom of the
pole so that it looks round.

**STEP 5**
Add any extra details.

**STEP 6**
Color.

# BUTTERFLIES

## Butterfly 1

**STEP 1**
Start with two connecting curved lines for the body and two curved lines for the antennae.

**STEP 2**
Draw overlapping curved lines on each side for the top wings.

**STEP 3**
Add a curved line below each wing for the bottom set. Color.

## Butterfly 2

**STEP 1**
Start with two connecting curved lines for the body and two curved lines for the antennae.

**STEP 2**
Draw a triangle shape with a curved edge on each side for the top wings.

**STEP 3**
Add a curved line below each wing for the bottom set. Color.

## Butterfly 3

**STEP 1**
Start with two connecting curved lines for the body and two curved lines for the antennae.

**STEP 2**
Add three connected curved lines on each side for the top wings.

**STEP 3**
Draw a smaller wing on each side, using two connected curved lines. Color.

# CACTUS

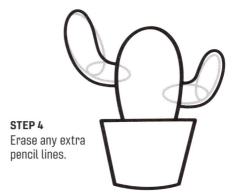

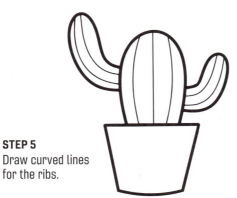

**STEP 1**
Start with a trapezoid. Curve the bottom so that it looks round for the pot.

**STEP 2**
Add a curved line coming out of the top of the pot.

**STEP 3**
Use ovals as guidelines to create two arms.

**STEP 4**
Erase any extra pencil lines.

**STEP 5**
Draw curved lines for the ribs.

**STEP 6**
Make straight lines for the prickles. Add any extra details and color.

# DRAGONFLY & LADYBUG

## Dragonfly

**STEP 1**
Start by stacking two ovals. The bottom oval should be slightly smaller.

**STEP 2**
Draw a long, skinny curved line underneath the ovals.

**STEP 3**
Use teardrop shapes for the wings and curved lines for the antennae. Color.

## Ladybug

**STEP 1**
Start with half an oval for the body.

**STEP 2**
Make a curved line for the head.

**STEP 3**
Fill in the body with circles for dots and draw two lines for antennae. Color.

 # FLOWERS

## Flower 1

**STEP 1**
Start with a circle for the center.

**STEP 2**
Draw connected curved lines around the circle.

**STEP 3**
Add details and color.

## Flower 2

**STEP 1**
Start with a circle for the center.

**STEP 2**
Draw a curved rectangle for each petal. Connect each petal to the circle.

**STEP 3**
Add details and color.

## Flower 3

**STEP 1**
Start with a circle for the center.

**STEP 2**
Draw a long, skinny curved line for each petal. Connect each petal to the circle.

**STEP 3**
Add details and color.

  # gNoMe

**STEP 1**
Draw a circle for the nose and a curved line behind it for the bottom of the hat.

**STEP 2**
Make a triangle guideline for the top of the hat.

**STEP 3**
Use wavy lines to complete the hat and a jagged, curved line connected to the hat for the beard.

**STEP 4**
Draw two ovals for the boots underneath the beard.

**STEP 5**
Use a rectangle to complete the body.

**STEP 6**
Add two curved lines for the arms.

 **STEP 7**
Add details and color.

# LEAF
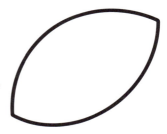

**STEP 1**
Start with a curved line.

**STEP 2**
Add another curved line connected to the first one.

**STEP 3**
Draw a straight line through the center.

**STEP 4**
Add diagonal lines for the veins and color.

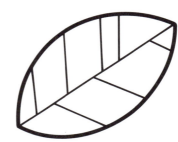

# MUSHROOM

**STEP 1**
Start with a curved line for the mushroom cap.

**STEP 2**
Close the cap with another curved line.

**STEP 3**
Draw a curved line connected to the cap for the stem.

**STEP 4**
Close the cap with another curved line.

**STEP 5**
Add details and color.

# PUMPKIN

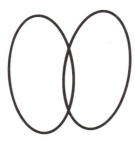

**STEP 1**
Start with two overlapping ovals.

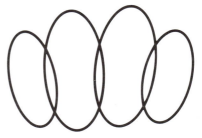

**STEP 2**
Add a smaller overlapping oval on each side.

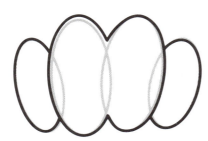

**STEP 3**
Erase any extra pencil lines.

**STEP 4**
Draw a curved rectangle for the stem.

**STEP 5**
Make curved lines for the ribs.

**STEP 6**
Add details and color.

# SEEDLINGS

**STEP 1**
Start with a skinny rectangle
for the lip of the pot.

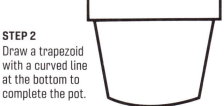

**STEP 2**
Draw a trapezoid
with a curved line
at the bottom to
complete the pot.

**STEP 3**
Make a wavy line coming from
the top of the pot for dirt.

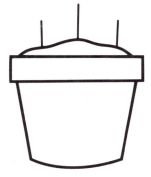

**STEP 4**
Add straight lines for stems.

**STEP 5**
Draw two leaves coming
from each stem.

**STEP 6**
Add details and color.

# SEED PACKET

**STEP 1**
Start with a slight trapezoid shape.

**STEP 2**
Use straight lines for the label.

**STEP 3**
Draw a wiggly line at the corner to show the packet has been ripped open.

**STEP 4**
Make ovals for seeds and draw a flower on the bottom of the packet. Color.

# SNOWFLAKES

**Snowflake 1**

**STEP 1**
Start with a circle as a guideline. Use intersecting lines to draw a star inside the circle.

**STEP 2**
Add an open triangle at the end of each line of the star.

**STEP 3**
Draw a smaller open triangle next to the first one on every other line and erase the guideline.

**Snowflake 2**

**STEP 1**
Start with a circle as a guideline. Draw a cross that touches the circle and a smaller intersecting X inside.

**STEP 2**
Add a small circle in the center of the snowflake and an open triangle on each cross line.

**STEP 3**
Continue adding open triangles on the cross lines and erase the guideline.

**Snowflake 3**

**STEP 1**
Start with a circle as a guideline. Use intersecting lines to draw a star inside and put a circle at each line's end.

**STEP 2**
Draw a smaller star in the center.

**STEP 3**
Use diagonal lines to connect each line of the smaller star. Erase the guideline.

# SNOWMAN

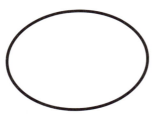

**STEP 1**
Start with an oval for the head.

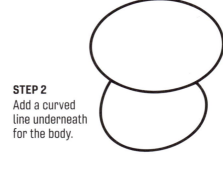

**STEP 2**
Add a curved line underneath for the body.

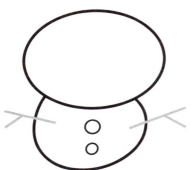

**STEP 3**
Draw two circles for buttons and two Ys for arms.

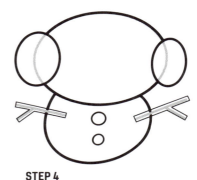

**STEP 4**
Trace around the arms to create sticks and make two circles on either side of the head for earmuffs.

**STEP 5**
Erase any extra pencil lines.

**STEP 6**
Connect the earmuffs with a curved line and add a face and any extra details. Color.

 # sTeMs

**STEP 1**
Start with a curved line.

**STEP 2**
Add curved diagonal lines to complete the branch.

**STEP 3**
Draw circles for leaves or berries.

**STEP 4**
Or add teardrop-shaped leaves.

**STEP 5**
Use connected teardrop shapes for flowers.

**STEP 6**
Or make curved lines for leaves.

**STEP 7**
Add details and color.

# SuCCuLeNTs

## Pot

**STEP 1**
Start with a skinny rectangle for the lip.

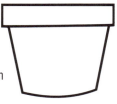

**STEP 2**
Draw a trapezoid with a curved line at the bottom to complete the pot.

## Succulent 1

**STEP 1**
Start with a curved line connected to the lip of the pot.

**STEP 2**
Add curved lines for the ribs and a flower on top.

**STEP 3**
Draw lines for the prickles and color.

## Succulent 2

**STEP 1**
Draw two overlapping curved lines connected to the lip of the pot.

**STEP 2**
Continue adding smaller curved lines.

**STEP 3**
Draw lines for the prickles and color.

## Succulent 3

**STEP 1**
Start with curved lines connected to the lip of the pot for the leaves.

**STEP 2**
Add more leaves behind the first ones you drew.

**STEP 3**
Add details and color.

# SUNSHINE

**STEP 1**
Start with a circle
for the center.

**STEP 2**
Draw straight lines
from the center
for the rays.

**STEP 3**
Or draw triangles
connected to the
center circle for a
different way to make the rays.

**STEP 4**
Or draw connected
curved lines around the
outside of the circle.

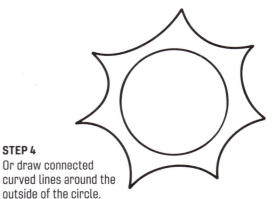

**STEP 5**
Add details
and color.

# TReeS

## Tree 1

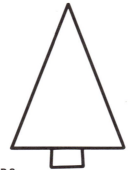

**STEP 1**
Start with a long, skinny triangle.

**STEP 2**
Draw a small rectangle connected to the triangle for the trunk.

**STEP 3**
Add details and color.

## Tree 2

**STEP 1**
Start with connected curved lines for the leaves.

**STEP 2**
Draw a long, skinny rectangle connected to the leaves for the trunk.

**STEP 3**
Add details and color.

# WATERING CAN

**STEP 1**
Start with an oval for the top.

**STEP 2**
Draw a trapezoid with a curved bottom underneath for the can.

**STEP 3**
Add another oval to the side of the can and an oval on the top.

**STEP 4**
Connect the side oval to the can with two diagonal lines.

**STEP 5**
Make double curved lines for the top handle and the side handle.

**STEP 6**
Add details and color!

  # PRACTICE

# FOOD DRAWINGS

# AVOCADO

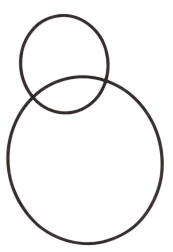

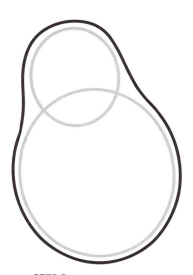

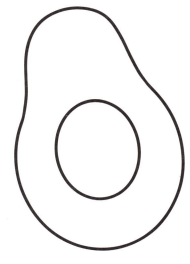

**STEP 1**
Start with two overlapping ovals for a base shape. The top oval should be slightly smaller.

**STEP 2**
Trace around the ovals.

**STEP 3**
Erase any extra pencil lines and add an oval for the center.

**STEP 4**
Add details and color.

# BUBBLE TEA

**STEP 1**
Start with a trapezoid.
Curve the bottom line.

**STEP 2**
Add a long, skinny rectangle
on top.

**STEP 3**
Draw a half circle on top
of the rectangle.

**STEP 4**
Make a straight line for the top of the drink
and add circles for the bubbles. Draw an
oval on the top for the straw opening.

**STEP 5**
Make a long, skinny rectangle with
a circle at the top for the straw.

**STEP 6**
Add details and color.

# CAKE

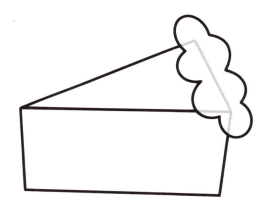

**STEP 1**
Start with a rectangle.

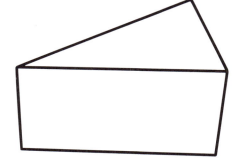

**STEP 2**
Draw a triangle on top.

**STEP 3**
Add connected curved lines along
the short end of the triangle.

**STEP 4**
Erase any extra pencil lines.
Use straight lines and curved
lines to create the layers.

**STEP 5**
Add details
and color.

# COFFEE

**STEP 1**
Start with a trapezoid.
Curve the bottom line.

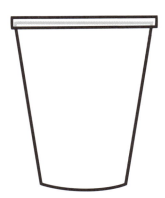

**STEP 2**
Add a long, skinny
rectangle on top.

**STEP 3**
Make another trapezoid on
top of the rectangle.

**STEP 4**
Draw a small oval inside
the top trapezoid.

**STEP 5**
Make a straight line and a slightly
curved line for the sleeve.

**STEP 6**
Add details and color.

# cookies

## Chocolate Chip

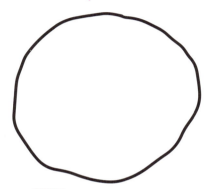

**STEP 1**
Start with a wavy circle.

**STEP 2**
Add connected curved lines
to make a bite mark.

**STEP 3**
Erase any extra pencil lines.
Add details and color.

## Macaron

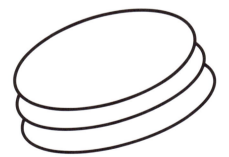

**STEP 1**
Start with an oval.

**STEP 2**
Add two curved lines underneath.

**STEP 3**
Add details and color.

# CROISSANT

**STEP 1**
Start with a curved line as
a guideline for the top.

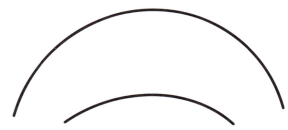

**STEP 2**
Make a smaller curved line
underneath for the bottom guideline.

**STEP 3**
Make a trapezoid in the center.
Curve the top and bottom to
follow the guidelines.

**STEP 4**
Add a rectangular shape on each
side, following the guidelines.

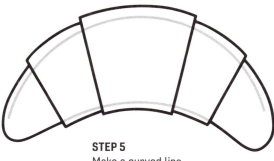

**STEP 5**
Make a curved line
at each end.

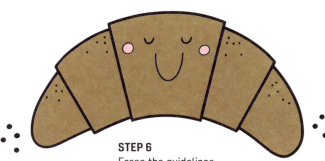

**STEP 6**
Erase the guidelines.
Add details and color.

# CUPCAKE

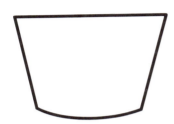

**STEP 1**
Start with a trapezoid. Curve the bottom.

**STEP 2**
Make an oval on the top.

**STEP 3**
Make connected curved lines at the bottom of the oval for the icing.

**STEP 4**
Erase any extra pencil lines and make a small paisley shape on top.

**STEP 5**
Draw an oval underneath the paisley.

**STEP 6**
Erase any extra pencil lines. Add details and color.

# DONUT

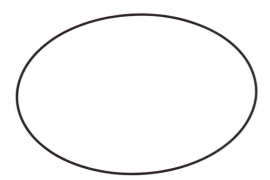

**STEP 1**
Start with an oval.

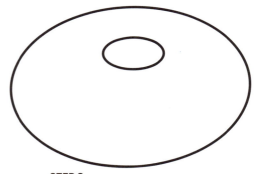

**STEP 2**
Make a smaller oval inside.

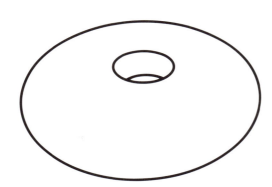

**STEP 3**
Draw a curved line inside the smaller oval.

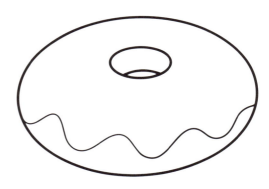

**STEP 4**
Make a wavy line for the frosting.

**STEP 5**
Add details and color.

# eggs & BACON

## Egg

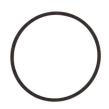

**STEP 1**
Start with a circle.

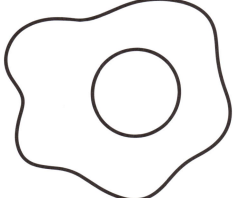

**STEP 2**
Draw a wavy circular
shape around it.

**STEP 3**
Add details and color.

## Bacon

**STEP 1**
Start with a wavy line.

**STEP 2**
Add 3 parallel wavy lines.
Close the top and bottom
with a straight line.

**STEP 3**
Add details and color.

# FRUIT

## Apple

**STEP 1**
Start with two
overlapping ovals.

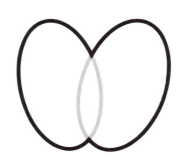

**STEP 2**
Erase any extra pencil lines.

**STEP 3**
Add a stem, leaf, and any
extra details. Color.

## Cherry

**STEP 1**
Start with two
overlapping ovals.

**STEP 2**
Erase any extra pencil lines.
Draw a long, curved line for
the stem.

**STEP 3**
Add details and color.

## Orange

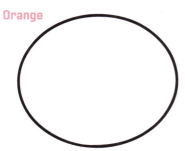

**STEP 1**
Start with an oval.

**STEP 2**
Add a small rectangle for the
stem and use curved lines to
make a leaf.

**STEP 3**
Add details and color.

## Watermelon

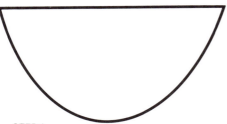

**STEP 1**
Start with half a circle.

**STEP 2**
Add connected curved lines to make a bite mark.

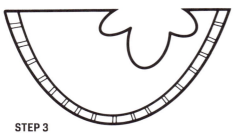

**STEP 3**
Erase any extra pencil lines. Add another half circle inside the first and draw straight stripes inside.

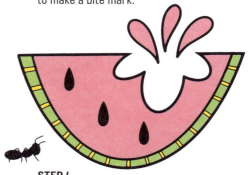

**STEP 4**
Add details and color.

## Blueberry

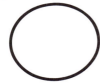

**STEP 1**
Start with a circle.

**STEP 2**
Use a circle and curved lines to draw a small flower toward the top.

**STEP 3**
Add details and color.

## Strawberry

**STEP 1**
Start with a rounded triangular shape.

**STEP 2**
Add connected curved lines for the stem.

**STEP 3**
Add details and color.

TRUST ME, YOU CAN DRAW

# HAMBURGER
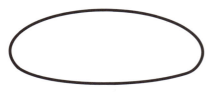
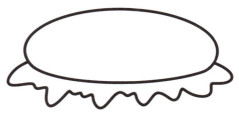

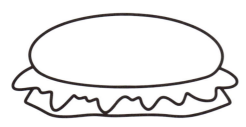

**STEP 1**
Start with an oval for the top of the bun.

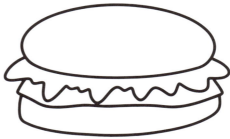

**STEP 2**
Draw a wavy line underneath for lettuce.

**STEP 3**
Make a wavy trapezoid underneath for the cheese.

**STEP 4**
Add a curved rectangular shape underneath for the meat.

**STEP 5**
Draw another curved line underneath for the bottom of the bun.

**STEP 6**
Add details and color.

# HOT Dog

**STEP 1**
Start with an oval for the bun.
Make a slight indent in the top.

**STEP 2**
Draw a line parallel to the top
of the bun for the hot dog.

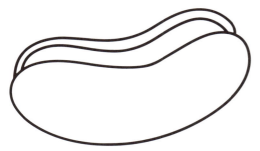

**STEP 3**
Add another longer parallel line behind
the hot dog for the back of the bun.

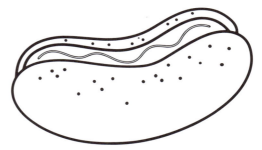

**STEP 4**
Add details and color.

# iCe CReAM

## Ice Cream

**STEP 1**
Start with a circle. Leave the bottom of the circle open.

**STEP 2**
Draw connected curved lines to finish the scoop.

## Sugar Cone

**STEP 1**
Draw a triangle from the bottom of the ice cream scoop.

**STEP 2**
Make a crisscross pattern inside the cone. Color.

## Cake Cone

**STEP 1**
Draw a rectangle shape coming from the scoop, with a square shape underneath. Curve the bottoms of these shapes.

**STEP 2**
Add a crisscross pattern in the bottom square and a curved line in the top rectangle. Color.

## STEP 1
Start with a trapezoid.

## STEP 2
Add a curved line on top.

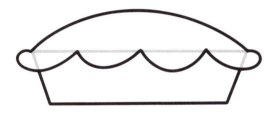

## STEP 3
Add connected curved lines at the bottom of the curved line.

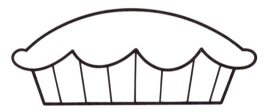

## STEP 4
Make straight lines for the bottom details.

## STEP 5
Add details and color.

# PiZZA

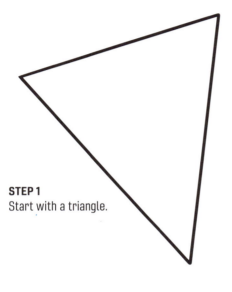

**STEP 1**
Start with a triangle.

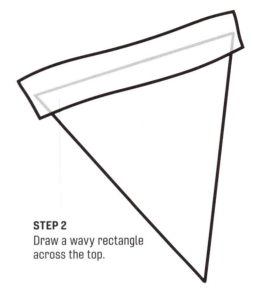

**STEP 2**
Draw a wavy rectangle
across the top.

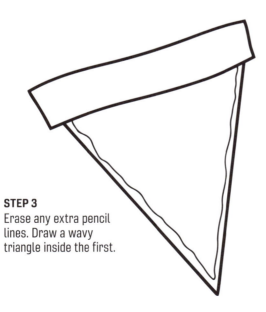

**STEP 3**
Erase any extra pencil
lines. Draw a wavy
triangle inside the first.

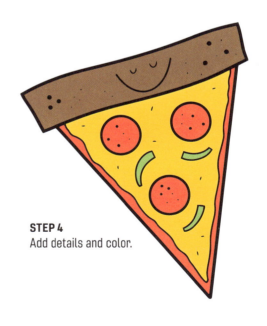

**STEP 4**
Add details and color.

# POPSICLE

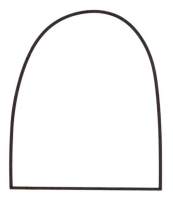

## STEP 1
Start with half an oval.

## STEP 2
Draw a smaller half oval underneath for the stick.

## STEP 3
Add connected curved lines for the bite.

## STEP 4
Add details and color.

 # SuSHi

## Roll 1

**STEP 1**
Start with an oval.

**STEP 2**
Draw two straight lines down from each side of the oval.

**STEP 3**
Use a curved line to connect the straight lines and add an oval inside the first one.

## Roll 2

**STEP 1**
Start with a curved, long, skinny rectangle.

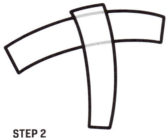

**STEP 2**
Draw another curved rectangle down from the center of the first.

**STEP 3**
Finish the roll with connected curved lines for the rice.

**STEP 4**
Add details and color.

**Roll 3**

**STEP 1**
Start with a long, skinny, curved line.

**STEP 2**
Draw a rectangular shape underneath.
Curve the bottom of the rectangle.

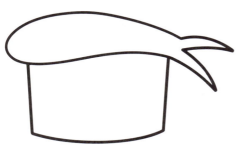

**STEP 3**
Add two skinny triangles for the tail.

**STEP 4**
Add details and color.

# TACO & JALAPEÑO

**Taco**

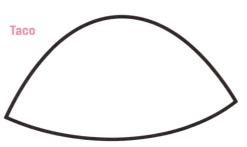

**STEP 1**
Start with half an oval. Curve the bottom line.

**STEP 2**
Make wavy lines on top.

**STEP 3**
Add another curved line behind the wavy lines for the back of the shell.

**STEP 4**
Add details and color.

**Jalepeño**

**STEP 1**
Start with a J shape. Draw a wiggly paisley shape around it.

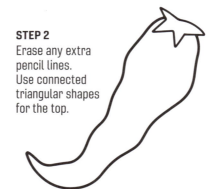

**STEP 2**
Erase any extra pencil lines. Use connected triangular shapes for the top.

**STEP 3**
Add details and color.

 # TOAST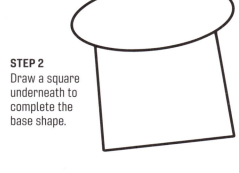

**STEP 1**
Start with an oval.

**STEP 2**
Draw a square
underneath to
complete the
base shape.

**STEP 3**
Trace around the base shape
and erase any extra pencil lines.

**STEP 4**
Trace around the main
shape with a wiggly line.

**STEP 5**
Add details
and color.

# Vegetables

## Carrot

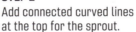

**STEP 1**
Start with a teardrop shape.

**STEP 2**
Add connected curved lines at the top for the sprout.

**STEP 3**
Add details and color.

## Broccoli

**STEP 1**
Draw connected curved lines in a circular shape. Leave the bottom open.

**STEP 2**
Use straight and curved lines for the stem.

**STEP 3**
Add details and color.

## Radish

**STEP 1**
Start with a paisley shape.

**STEP 2**
Add two curved lines from the top. Surround the top of those lines with connected curved lines for the leaves.

**STEP 3**
Add details and color.

# PRACTICE

# SUPER FUN DRAWINGS

# BANNERS

## Banner 1

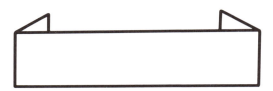

**STEP 1**
Start with a long, skinny rectangle.

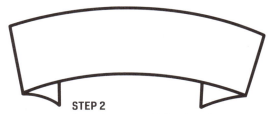

**STEP 2**
Draw a triangle at the top of each side of the rectangle.

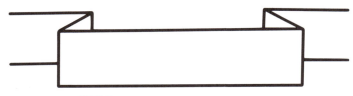

**STEP 3**
Make straight lines extending from the top of each triangle and straight lines extending from each side of the rectangle.

**STEP 4**
Close off each side with connected curved lines. Add details and color.

## Banner 2

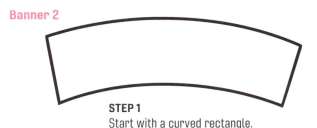

**STEP 1**
Start with a curved rectangle.

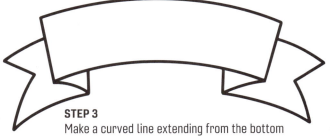

**STEP 2**
Draw two curved triangles at the bottom of each side.

**STEP 3**
Make a curved line extending from the bottom of each triangle and another curved line extending from each side of the rectangle. Close off each side with an open triangle.

**STEP 4**
Add details and color.

# BASEBALL GLOVE

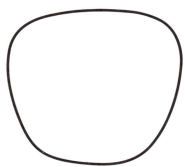

**STEP 1**
Start with a curved trapezoid.

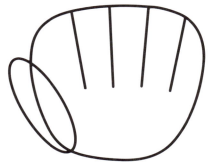

**STEP 2**
Draw an oval on the side and four straight lines from the top.

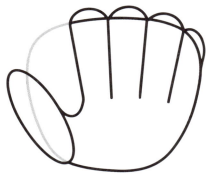

**STEP 3**
Connect each straight line with a curved line and use another curved line to connect the side oval.

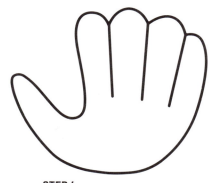

**STEP 4**
Erase all extra pencil lines.

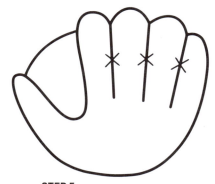

**STEP 5**
Connect the thumb with a curved line and draw an X on the center of each straight line.

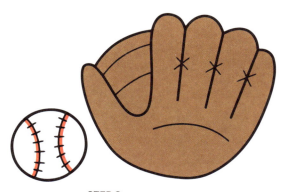

**STEP 6**
Add details and color.

# BOOM BOX

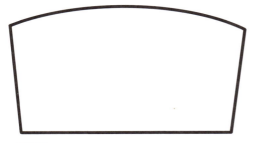

## STEP 1
Start with a rectangle shape.
Curve the top line of the rectangle.

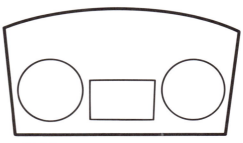

## STEP 2
Draw two circles for speakers
and a rectangle for a tape deck.

## STEP 3
Use a curved line connected by straight
lines for the handle.

## STEP 4
Add small squares, circles, and another
rectangle with a curved top to decorate
the front and top.

## STEP 5
Make a straight line with an oval on top for
an antenna. Use circles, straight lines, and
a trapezoid to complete the tape deck.

## STEP 6
Add details and color.

# CAMPER

### STEP 1
Start with two circles for the wheel.

### STEP 2
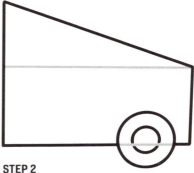

Draw a rectangle behind the wheel and a triangle on top of the rectangle.

### STEP 3

Trace around the rectangle and triangle with a curved line.

### STEP 4
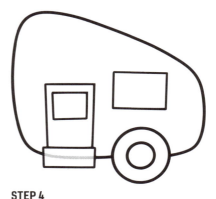

Erase any extra pencil lines and use rectangles to make the door and window.

### STEP 5

Make a hitch with straight lines and an oval. Make a spare tire on the back with curved lines.

### STEP 6

Add details and color.

 # CLOUDS

## Happy Cloud

**STEP 1**
Start with two connected curved lines.

**STEP 2**
Continue adding curved lines in the shape of an oval. Add a face and color.

## Rainbow Cloud

**STEP 1**
Start with a cloud. Add a curved line connected to the top.

**STEP 2**
Continue adding curved lines underneath the first. Add details and color.

## Lightning Cloud

**STEP 1**
Start with a cloud. Add two angled L lines extending from the bottom.

**STEP 2**
Connect the edges of the L lines with angled lines. Add details and color.

# CRAYON

**STEP 1**
Start with a long, skinny rectangle.
Curve one end.

**STEP 2**
Add a rectangle on the end
with the straight edge.

**STEP 3**
Make a small oval to the
side of the rectangle.

**STEP 4**
Connect the oval to the rectangle
with angled lines.

**STEP 5**
Draw an oval in the center and
double curved lines for the label.

**STEP 6**
Add details
and color.

# envelope & letter

**STEP 1**
Start with a rectangle.

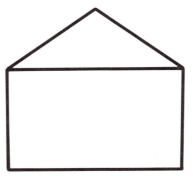

**STEP 2**
Draw a triangle on the top.

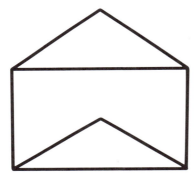

**STEP 3**
Make another triangle at the bottom.

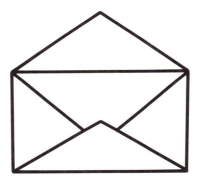

**STEP 4**
Use two angled lines to connect the top corners of the rectangle to the bottom triangle.

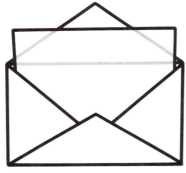

**STEP 5**
Draw a rectangular shape from the top of the envelope base for the letter.

**STEP 6**
Erase any extra pencil lines.
Add details and color.

# FEATHER

**STEP 1**
Start with a curved line.

**STEP 2**
Draw two curved lines at the top.

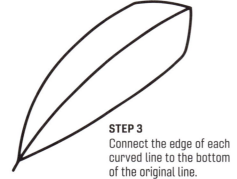

**STEP 3**
Connect the edge of each curved line to the bottom of the original line.

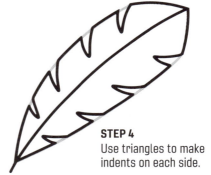

**STEP 4**
Use triangles to make indents on each side.

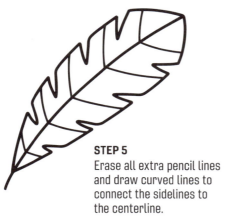

**STEP 5**
Erase all extra pencil lines and draw curved lines to connect the sidelines to the centerline.

**STEP 6**
Add a pattern inside and color.

# FRAMES

## Frame 1

**STEP 1**
Start with a trapezoid.

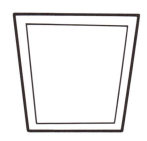

**STEP 2**
Draw another trapezoid inside the first.

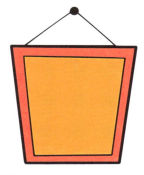

**STEP 3**
Make a triangle with a circle at the top for a hanger. Color.

## Frame 2

**STEP 1**
Start with a rectangle.

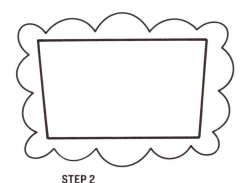

**STEP 2**
Make connected curved lines around the outside.

**STEP 3**
Add details and color.

## Frame 3

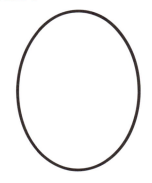

**STEP 1**
Start with an oval.

**STEP 2**
Add curved lines in a symmetrical pattern around the outside.

**STEP 3**
Outline the outside of the curved lines and draw another oval inside the first one. Color.

 # gemstone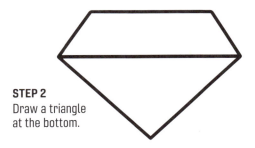

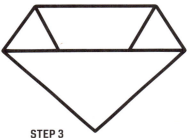

**STEP 1**
Start with a trapezoid.

**STEP 2**
Draw a triangle
at the bottom.

**STEP 3**
Make two small triangles
coming from the points of
the top of the trapezoid.

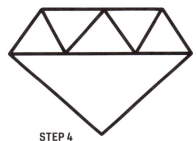

**STEP 4**
Draw another triangle
in the center to connect
the two triangles.

**STEP 5**
Make two angled lines from the
bottom of the center triangle
to connect to the bottom point.

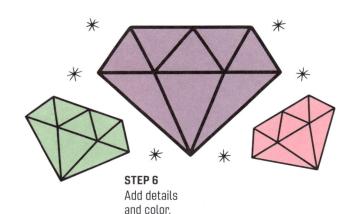

**STEP 6**
Add details
and color.

# HOUSE

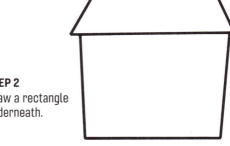

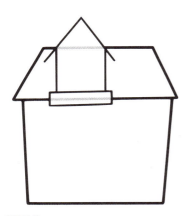

**STEP 1**
Start with a trapezoid
for the roof.

**STEP 2**
Draw a rectangle
underneath.

**STEP 3**
Make a rectangle for a windowsill and
another rectangle with a triangle for
the top to of the window.

**STEP 4**
Double the line for the top of the
window and use rectangles to make a
door, chimney, and additional window.

**STEP 5**
Draw straight lines for siding
and a cross in each window.

**STEP 6**
Erase any extra pencil lines.
Add details and color.

# LIGHTBULB

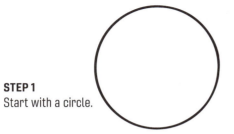

**STEP 1**
Start with a circle.

**STEP 2**
Draw an overlapping trapezoid at the bottom.

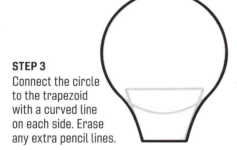

**STEP 3**
Connect the circle to the trapezoid with a curved line on each side. Erase any extra pencil lines.

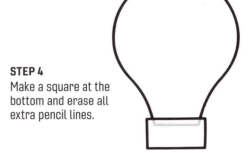

**STEP 4**
Make a square at the bottom and erase all extra pencil lines.

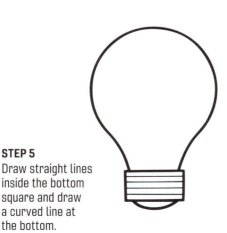

**STEP 5**
Draw straight lines inside the bottom square and draw a curved line at the bottom.

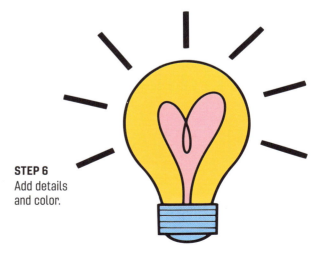

**STEP 6**
Add details and color.

# MOON & STAR

**STEP 1**
Start with a
curved line.

**STEP 2**
Draw a backward
L from the top of
the curved line to
make the nose.

**STEP 3**
Use a curved line
to connect the
bottom of the nose
to the bottom of
the curved line.

**STEP 4**
Make a face on the
moon. Draw a star
and trace around
the outside.

**STEP 5**
Erase any extra pencil lines.
Add details and color.

# PAINTBRUSHES

**Watercolor Brush**

**STEP 1**
Start with two long, curved lines for the handle. Connect them with a curved line at the top.

**STEP 2**
Draw two connecting lines for the brush.

**Tempera Brush**

**STEP 1**
Start with two long, curved lines for the handle. Connect them with a curved line at the top.

**STEP 2**
Draw straight lines for the bristles.

**STEP 3**
Add details and color.

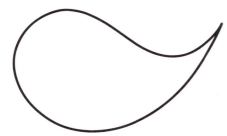 # PAISLEY

**STEP 1**
Start with a paisley shape.

**STEP 2**
Make another, smaller paisley inside.

**STEP 3**
Draw curved lines around the outside of both paisleys.

**STEP 4**
Add a flower and leaf inside the center of the inside paisley and draw smaller curved lines inside each curved line.

**STEP 5**
Use straight lines to add stripes to the inside.

**STEP 6**
Color.

# PENCIL & SHARPENER

## Pencil

**STEP 1**
Start with two angled lines.
Connect them with straight lines.

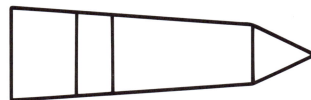

**STEP 2**
Add two straight lines for the
ferrule and a triangle for the top.

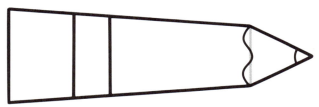

**STEP 3**
Make a curved line at the end of
the triangle for the pencil point.
Draw a wavy line where the top connects.

## Sharpener

**STEP 1**
Start with a rectangle.

**STEP 2**
Draw curved lines for the side grips
and the section where the blade is.

**STEP 3**
Erase any extra pencil lines and add
straight lines at the edge and a tiny
circle with an X inside for the screw.

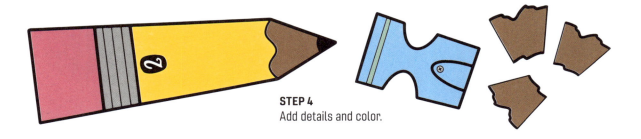

**STEP 4**
Add details and color.

# ROBOT

**STEP 1**
Start by drawing a
trapezoid for the head.

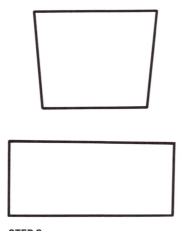

**STEP 2**
Add a rectangle underneath
for the body.

**STEP 3**
Connect the head and body with a
rectangle and draw two rectangles
for legs. Use a square and
rectangles for the inside controls.

**STEP 4**
Draw curved
lines for the
arms and feet.

**STEP 5**
Add details
and color.

# ROCKET

**STEP 1**
Start with a tall trapezoid shape.

**STEP 2**
Make a triangle on top.

**STEP 3**
Draw a triangle on each side for the wings.

**STEP 4**
Curve the edge of each triangle. Draw a circle for the window and two small trapezoids for the boosters.

**STEP 5**
Erase any extra pencil lines. Add details and color.

# SUGAR SKULL

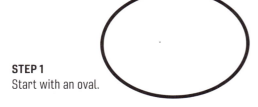

**STEP 1**
Start with an oval.

**STEP 2**
Add a trapezoid
underneath.

**STEP 3**
Erase any extra
pencil lines. Draw
ovals for eyes, an
upside-down heart
for the nose, and a
curved line at the
top.

**STEP 4**
Make a straight
line for the
mouth and angled
intersecting lines
for the teeth.

**STEP 5**
Draw curved lines
around the eyes
and top to
create petals.

**STEP 6**
Add details
and color.

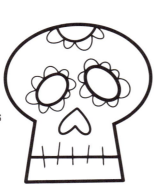

# UNiCORN

### STEP 1
Start with a jelly bean shape for the body.

### STEP 2
Draw an oval above for the head.

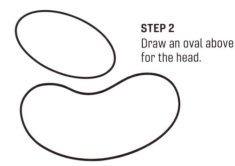

### STEP 3
Connect the body and head and draw two rectangular shapes for legs.

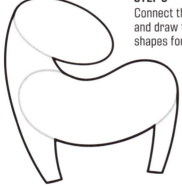

### STEP 4
Draw paisley shapes for the mane and tail.

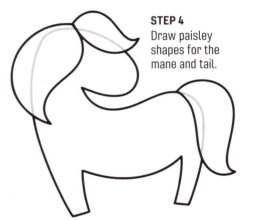

### STEP 5
Make triangular shapes for the horn and ear and a curved line on the head.

### STEP 6
Add details and color.

# PRACTICE

 # PRACTICE

# PRACTICE

LETTER

ABC

Learning to letter involves the same process as learning to draw. You start by combining lines and shapes. Then, you have to practice! Here are some tips to give your letters a fun look.

ABC → ABC

**Stagger letters for a whimsical look.**

A → AA    B → BB

**Change up crossbars and proportions to make letters look unique.**

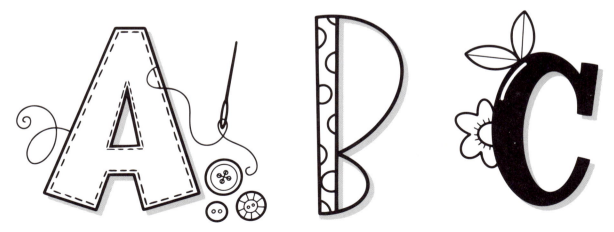

**Embellish letters with patterns and doodles.**

ART DECO LETTERS

These tall, skinny letters look great filled in with a solid color or even a pattern. Their shape makes them easy to fit into tight spaces.

ABCDEFG
HIJKLM
NOPQRST
UVWXYZ

Practice your letters here.

Practice your letters here.

G G G    H H H    I I I

Practice your letters here.

M  N  O

M  N  O

M  N  O

Practice your letters here.

S          T          U

S          T          U

S          T          U

Practice your letters here.

Practice your letters here.

y
y
y

Z
Z
Z

Practice your letters here.

abcdef
ghijklm
nopqrst
uvwxyz

Bubble letters are my favorite! You can fill them in with a solid color or put a pattern, like stripes or polka dots, inside. You can also embellish them with flowers or leaves. Try staggering your letters when you write a word to create a fun look.

Practice your letters here.

Practice your letters here.

Practice your letters here.

Practice your letters here.

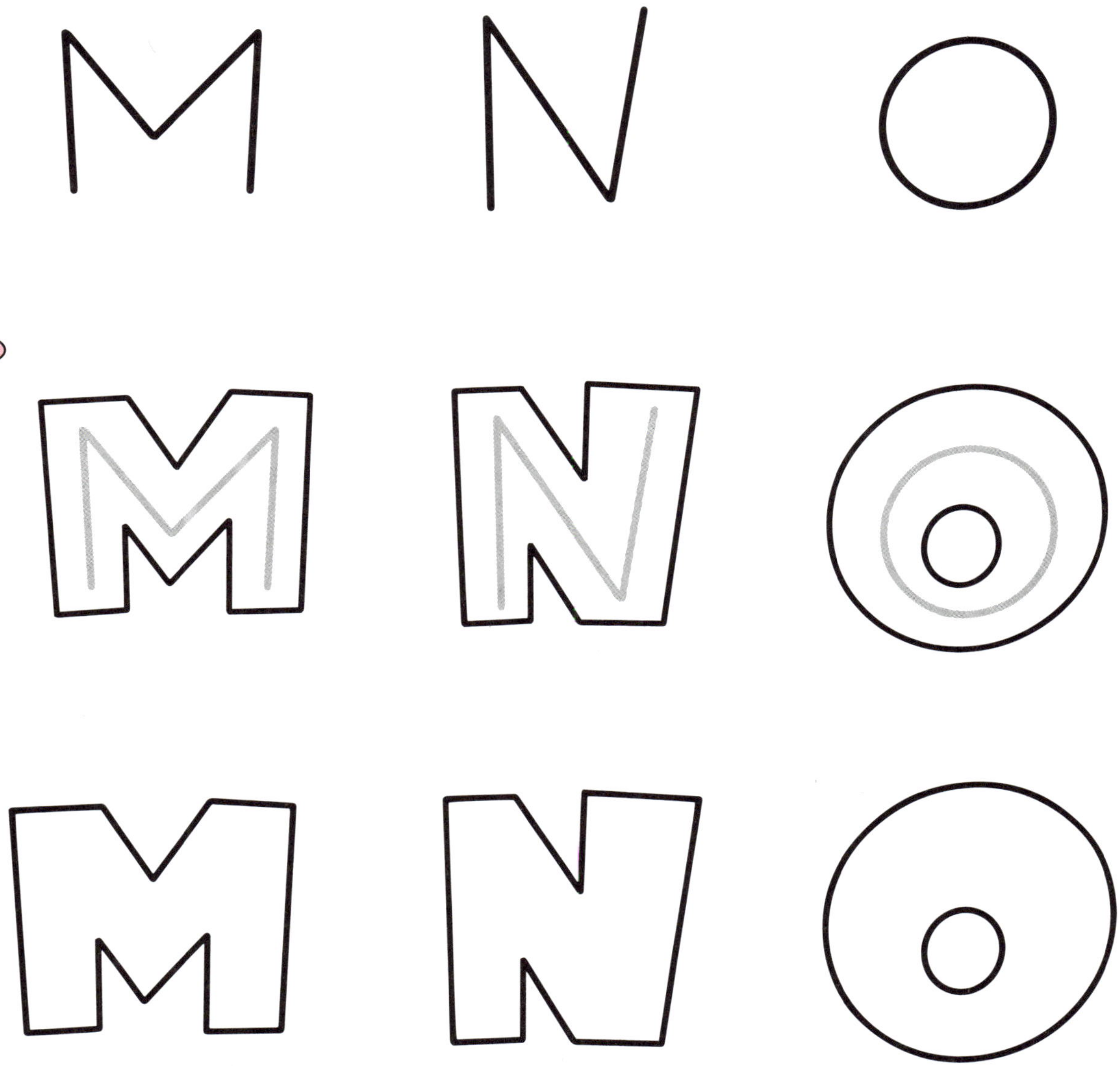

M N O

M N O

M N O

146

Practice your letters here.

Practice your letters here.

S  T  U

S  T  U

S  T  U

Practice your letters here.

Practice your letters here.

Practice your letters here.

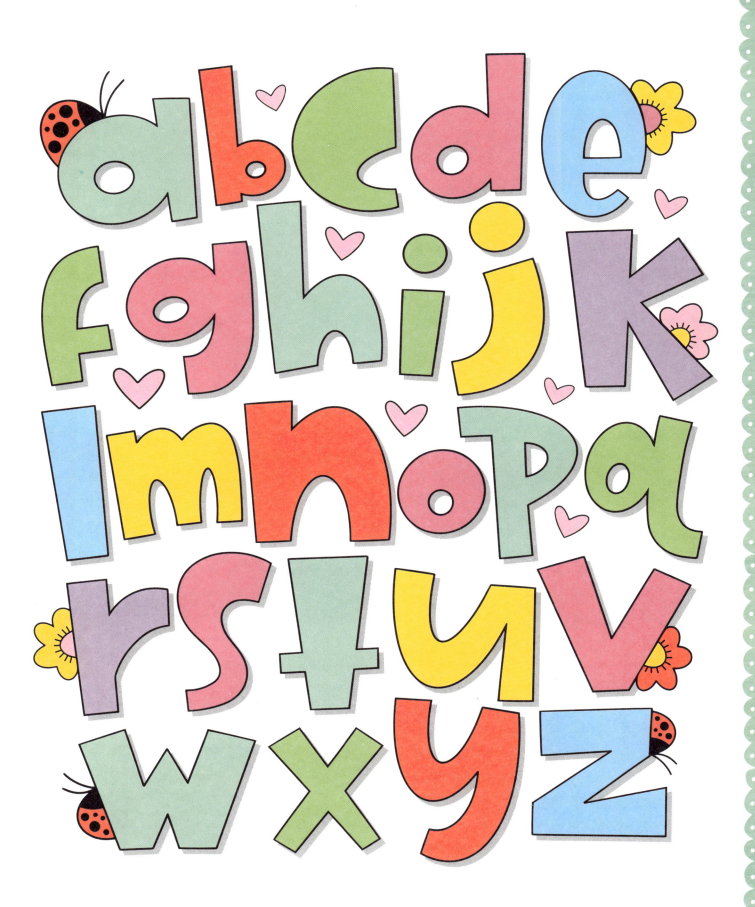

# SERiF LETTeRS

Serif letters are named for the small lines (feet) found at the ends of the letters. You can leave off these feet to easily create a sans serif style. Both styles are great for a bold look that will stand out in any design.

ABCDEF
GHiJK
LMNoPQ
RSTUV
WXYZ

A B C

A B C

A B C

Practice your letters here.

D E F

D E F

D E F

Practice your letters here.

G H i

G H i

G H i

Practice your letters here.

J K L

**J** **K** **L**

J K L

M N O

M N O

M N O

Practice your letters here.

P Q R

P Q R

P Q R

S T U

S T U

S T U

Practice your letters here.

abcdef
ghijk
lmnopq
rstuv
wxyz

 # PRACTICE

# PRACTICE

# PUTTING iT ALL together

Hooray!
You have reached the last chapter of the book.
At this point, you know how to draw, and you know how
to letter. Now, it's time to put it all together.

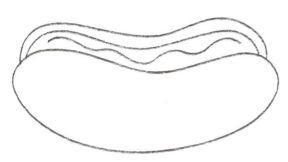

**STEP 1**
Sketch your drawing.

**STEP 2**
Decide which style of lettering you would like to use.
It's okay to use more than one!

**STEP 3**
Trace over your drawing with ink
and erase any extra pencil lines.

**STEP 4**
Add details, shadows, and highlights to add drama to your design.
Then, fill in any extra spaces with doodle fillers. I used stars for
the example above. Finish your design with color!

**Why did the watermelons want a big wedding?**
Because they cantaloupe.

# LOOKING SHARP

Did you hear the story about the broken pencil?

I'd tell you but there's no point.

**Why is baseball the gnomes' favorite sport?**
Because they love to score gnome runs.

What kind of books do owls like to read?
Hoo-dunits!

What do you call a beehive with no way out?

Un-Bee-Leave-Able

Why do birthday candles go on top of the cake?

Because it's hard to blow them out on the bottom!

PLANT
ONE ON ME

What do you call it when two flowers are dating?

A budding romance.

best 4eas

Why is a good friend like a four-leaf clover?

They are hard to find!

# BETTER DAY BOOKS™
### HAPPY · CREATIVE · CURATED™

Business is personal at Better Day Books. We were founded on the belief that all people are creative and that making things by hand is inherently good for us. It's important to us that you know how much we appreciate your support. The book you are holding in your hands was crafted with the artistic passion of the author and brought to life by a team of wildly enthusiastic creatives who believed it could inspire you. If it did, please drop us a line and let us know about it. Connect with us on Instagram, post a photo of your art, and let us know what other creative pursuits you are interested in learning about. It all matters to us. You're kind of a big deal.

*it's a good day to have a better day!*™

www.betterdaybooks.com

better_day_books